TECHNOLOGY IN ANCIENT CULTURES

ANCIENT COMPUTING TECHNOLOGY

FROM ABACUSES TO WATER CLOCKS

Michael Woods and
Mary B. Woods

Twenty-First Century Books · Minneapolis

To Natalie and Jerome Gavin

Twenty-First Century Books
A division of Lerner Publishing Group, Inc.
241 First Avenue North
Minneapolis, MN 55401 U.S.A.

Website address: www.lernerbooks.com

Library of Congress Cataloging-in-Publication Data

Woods, Michael, 1946-
     Ancient computing technology : from abacuses to water clocks / by Michael Woods and Mary B. Woods.
        p.   cm. — (Technology in ancient cultures)
     Includes bibliographical references and index.
     ISBN 978-0-7613-6528-0 (lib. bdg. : alk. paper)
     1. Mathematics, Ancient—Juvenile literature. 2. Counting—Methodology—History—To 1500—Juvenile literature.
     I. Woods, Mary B. (Mary Boyle), 1946- II. Title.
     QA22.W664 2011
     510.28'4—dc22   2010027927

Manufactured in the United States of America
1 – PC – 12/31/10

TABLE OF CONTENTS

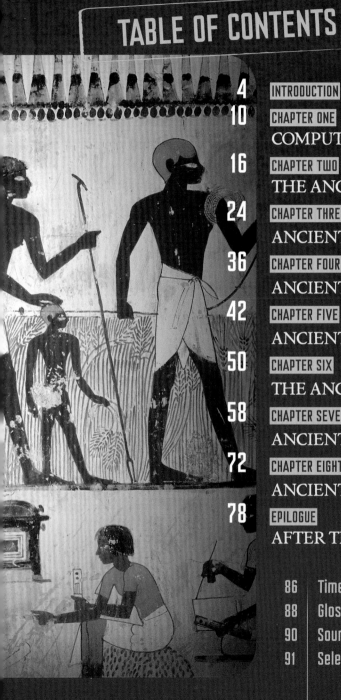

THE ANCIENT WORLDS OF COMPUTING

INTRODUCTION

What do you think of when you hear the word *technology*? You probably think of state-of-the-art gadgets. You might think of computers, mp3 players, and the latest scientific tools. But technology doesn't mean just brand-new machines and discoveries. Technology is as old as human civilization.

Technology is the use of knowledge, inventions, and discoveries to make life better. The word *technology* comes from two Greek words. One, *techne*, means "art" or "craft." The other, *logos*, means "word" or "speech." The ancient Greeks used the word *technology* to mean a discussion of arts and crafts. In modern times, *technology* refers to a craft, a technique, or a tool itself.

People use many kinds of technology. Medicine is one kind of technology. Construction and agriculture are also kinds of technologies. These technologies and many others make life easier, safer, and happier. This book looks at a form of technology used in almost every area of daily life and every field of science. That technology is computing.

WHAT IS COMPUTING?

When people hear the word *computing*, they usually think about using computers. But *computing* has another meaning. Computing involves using numbers to count, gather information, and solve problems. Computing also involves manipulating numbers by adding, subtracting, multiplying, and dividing them. Computing can be as simple as 1 + 1 = 2, or it can require the help of advanced calculators or computers.

Computing involves mathematics—the science of numbers. Math has many branches and many practical applications. It is used in almost every area of science, medicine, business, construction, and manufacturing.

▲ A boy completes a simple arithmetic problem on a chalkboard. For thousands of years, people have crunched numbers to make sense of the world.

▲ Over time, computer scientists were able to build advanced computing technology into devices that fit in a person's hand.

ANCIENT ROOTS

Computing probably began shortly after the first humans appeared on Earth. Early peoples performed mathematics by counting on their fingers and toes. They kept track of numbers by cutting notches into sticks and tying knots in ropes. This first computing technology was simple, yet it was effective, easy to learn, and accurate.

Ancient peoples discovered some computing methods by trial and error. Sometimes people copied and improved on computing technology used in other parts of the world. The ancient Greeks, for instance, learned about geometry from the Egyptians and the Babylonians. The Romans learned from the Greeks. Each civilization added improvements. Gradually, computing knowledge spread throughout the world. Mathematics became a universal language.

▲ An ancient Egyptian ruler from between 700 and 330 B.C. is marked with notches and number symbols.

Archaeologists are scientists who study the remains of past cultures. They learn about ancient computing knowledge through writings and carvings the ancients left behind. For example, the Rhind Papyrus, an ancient Egyptian text, was found in the 1850s. It was like a textbook, containing more than eighty mathematical problems. From these problems, modern archaeologists saw how ancient Egyptian students learned arithmetic and geometry around 1650 B.C.

Ancient tools and monuments can give clues about computing knowledge too. Greek water clocks showed how precisely the Greeks could tell time. In Central America, dates inscribed on stone monuments give insight to the calendar systems of the Mayan culture. Clues like these tell scientists how ancient peoples counted, measured, or calculated.

A LOT WITH A LITTLE

Ancient peoples performed very effective computations without smartphones or even pocket calculators. Most of the major branches of mathematics started in ancient times. Ancient engineers and builders used math to design roads, buildings, machines, and weapons.

Ancient computing has stood the test of time. We measure angles in degrees, minutes, and seconds thanks to the ancient Babylonians. We divide our day into twenty-four hours, just as the ancient Egyptians did. Our number symbols were created in ancient India. We sometimes use Roman numerals, developed in Rome more than two thousand years ago.

Ancient people used math for fun too. They developed number games, tricks, and puzzles. Read on and discover many wonders about the computing knowledge we inherited from people who lived long ago.

CHAPTER ONE

COMPUTING BASICS

▲ This cave painting from prehistoric Mexico was painted in around 7500 B.C. The human figures are shown with hands and fingers raised. Early peoples probably used fingers and toes to keep track of quantities.

The first humans on Earth lived about 2.5 million years ago. They were hunters and gatherers. They lived in small groups and got their food by hunting game, fishing, and gathering wild plants. When the food in one area was all used up, the group moved to a new place. Hunter-gatherers made tools from stone, wood, animal bones, plant fibers, and clay. In some places

on Earth, the hunter-gatherer lifestyle remained unchanged until only a few centuries ago.

Early hunters and gatherers probably knew the importance of quantities, or amounts. They knew that two antelopes meant more food than one. A pack of wolves was more dangerous than a lone wolf. A bunch of berries was more valuable than one berry. But did early hunter-gatherers understand the ideas behind numbers?

FINGER SYMBOLS AND STICKS

We can only guess about when humans developed basic systems for counting. They probably used fingers to represent numbers, just as young children do when they learn to count. One finger was probably the universal symbol for 1, two fingers for 2, and three for 3. For hunter-gatherers, four extended fingers might have stood for four woolly mammoths hiding just out of sight.

▲ When children first learn how to add and subtract, they often count on their fingers.

> **"Carefully notched bones from a 35,000-year-old level [of Border Cave in Swaziland], which may have been used to record phases of the moon, indicate that man had learned to count."**

—Ronald Schiller, "New Findings on the Origin of Man," 1973, discussing the Lebombo bone

It's no surprise that our modern numbering system is based on 10—the number of human fingers. In fact, the word *digit*, meaning a single numeral, also refers to a finger or toe.

STICKS AND BONES

Ancient peoples kept track of numbers with notches cut into sticks. Archaeologists have found ancient tally sticks. These were sticks and bones with rows of neatly cut notches. A tally stick known as the Lebombo bone was carved about 35,000 B.C. It was a baboon bone discovered near a cave in Swaziland, in southern Africa, in the 1970s. Twenty-nine notches were carved into the bone.

In 1960 archaeologists in central Africa had found a notched bone they called the Ishango bone. At first they thought this bone, carved in about

▲ The Ishango bone *(front and back shown)* is a tally stick that dates to around 20,000 B.C. This bone from a baboon's upper thigh is carved with notches. Archaeologists found the bone in 1960 in central Africa.

20,000 B.C., was a tally stick. But others believe its grouped notches stand for a pattern of some sort—possibly a calendar of the moon's phases.

MEASURING WITH BODY PARTS

In addition to counting on fingers, ancient peoples also measured with the human body. They used their feet to measure distances. For thousands of years, the foot—equal to 12 inches (30 centimeters) in modern times—was not a fixed length. It varied by as much as several inches, depending on the size of the human foot doing the measurement.

One of the most widely used ancient units of measurement was the cubit. It was the distance from a man's elbow to the end of his middle finger. At first, one inch was the width of a man's thumb. Later, one inch meant the length of an index finger from the tip to the first joint. The hand was the width of a man's hand—about 4 inches (10 cm). People still use hands to measure horses.

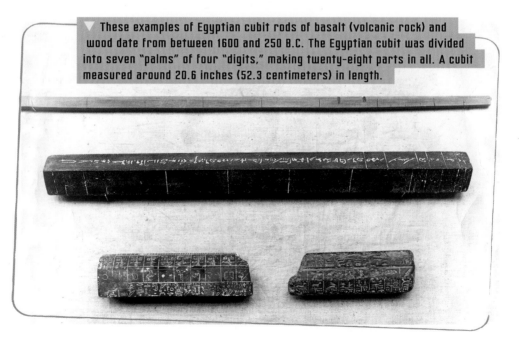

These examples of Egyptian cubit rods of basalt (volcanic rock) and wood date from between 1600 and 250 B.C. The Egyptian cubit was divided into seven "palms" of four "digits," making twenty-eight parts in all. A cubit measured around 20.6 inches (52.3 centimeters) in length.

MANCALA

Some ancient peoples used counting skills to play games. In the African countries of Eritrea and Ethiopia, scientists have found evidence of *mancala* games from the A.D. 500s or 600s.

A common version of these games uses two rows of six holes, or cups. Two larger holes sit at the ends. Players place stones, beans, or other small counters in the holes one by one. They follow certain rules to capture the counters. The player to capture the most counters wins. Skilled players use counting and calculating to determine their best move.

Versions of these games are still played around the world. They are known by many different names, including *wari* and *ayo*.

▲ The counting game of *ayo* (a version of *mancala*) is still popular among players in Nigeria.

Body-part measurements were not uniform. They varied a lot from person to person. But they did offer a big benefit—ancient people always had a ruler handy. In fact, some body-part measurements are still in use. In Southeast Asia, traditional Malay people use fingernails, handfuls, and the distance around a person's forearm as units of measurement.

CHAPTER TWO

THE ANCIENT MIDDLE EAST

Around 3500 B.C., some people in the Middle East began abandoning the hunter-gatherer lifestyle. Over time they started building houses, farms, and villages. They farmed fertile land between the Tigris and Euphrates rivers. This region was known as Mesopotamia (between rivers). Mesopotamia was home to many ancient cultures over several thousand years. These included the Sumerians, Babylonians, Hittites, and Assyrians.

Farmers in the ancient Middle East needed methods for counting crops, measuring land, and keeping track of the growing season. Because they traded crops and other goods with other groups of people, they needed scales and standard measurements.

As people in the Middle East settled into farming villages, they needed ways to mark the boundaries of their land. They developed a technology called surveying.

▼ This relief carving from the Assyrian Palace at Nineveh (in modern-day Iraq), ca. 650 B.C., shows farmers harvesting sugarcane on the banks of a river. People of the ancient Middle East used numbers and computing techniques to calculate sizes of plots of land.

Surveying uses math to measure distances, angles, and contours (curves) of land. With surveying techniques, people could determine areas and borders of farmers' plots of land. Ancient mapmakers could accurately show rivers, hills, and other land features on maps. Surveying was also important in construction. It helped ancient engineers design straight roads, buildings, and bridges.

Writings and other artifacts from the Sumerians show that people in the ancient Middle East measured land boundaries as early as 1400 B.C. The Sumerians also used careful measurement and surveying techniques to create building plans for their cities.

THE FIRST MAPS

Maps show the distances between cities, roads, and land features such as mountains and rivers. Mapmaking requires very precise measurement. Mapmakers must draw to scale, meaning distances on maps are in proportion to distances in the real world. For instance, 1 inch (2.5 cm) on a map may equal 10 miles (16 kilometers) on land.

The ancient Babylonians drew the first known maps in about 2300 B.C. They carved them in wet clay to make clay tablets. Many of these maps were legal records of landownership. They showed the size of farmers' fields. Other maps were guides for people on long journeys.

One Babylonian map, drawn around 600 B.C., showed the entire world—or at least what the Babylonians thought was the entire world. It showed the city of Babylon in the center, the Persian Gulf off to one side, and a few other countries, such as modern-day Armenia. All the land was surrounded by a huge ocean.

▼ This Babylonian map of the world, carved in a clay tablet in around 600 B.C., is on view at the British Museum in London, England.

THE FIRST SALESPEOPLE

Farmers in the ancient Middle East were perhaps the world's first salespeople. Mesopotamia contained excellent farmland. Farmers produced more food than they needed. So they were able to sell the surplus.

Babylon was a commercial center. At markets, merchants traded grain, dried fish, cloth, brick, and gold with people from many other cities. To charge and pay the same amount for identical amounts of goods, merchants needed standard units of money, length, and weight.

The cubit, the distance from a man's elbow to the tip of his middle finger, was a widely used unit of length in the ancient world. The Mesopotamians divided the cubit into smaller units. One cubit contained two feet. One foot contained three hands—the distance across a man's hand from index finger to little finger. A "finger's width" was equal to about 1 inch (2.5 cm).

COMPUTING WEIGHT

Archaeologists are not sure whether the first scale was invented in ancient Babylonia or in ancient Egypt. Both civilizations used scales, perhaps as early as 5000 B.C.

Ancient scales were beam scales. They were made from a stick or a rod balanced upon a center support. A pan hung from each end of the beam. When an object in one pan (a piece of gold, perhaps) was heavier than an object in the other, one pan hung lower. When the objects were equal in weight, the pans balanced.

▲ A funeral stone from a Hittite tomb in northern Syria depicts a merchant carrying a pair of beam scales. The stone was carved in the 800s B.C.

▲ This smooth set of standard weights was used in beam scales in Ur (modern-day southern Iraq) in 1900–1600 B.C. The weights are made from a stone called hematite.

The first beam scales simply compared the weight of two different objects. They didn't measure an object's weight based on standard units. The Babylonians eventually developed the world's first weight standards—units of measurement that were the same from place to place.

The Babylonian standards were smooth stones. They were ground and polished to make sure each weighed the same. Merchants placed one or more stones on one pan of a beam scale. They placed objects to be bought or sold in the other. They might have weighed out two stones' worth of grain, for example. With standardized weights, business transactions were made more accurate.

The beam scales used in Babylon may seem primitive. But scientists and others still use similar scales.

COMPUTING TIME

Sundials are devices that measure time by the position of the Sun as it moves across the sky. Sundials can be very accurate timekeepers. Of course, they aren't useful at night or on cloudy days. But sundials helped ancient peoples to measure daylight.

Some of the first sundials were made in ancient Babylonia. They were flat pieces of stone or wood with an upright bar called a gnomon. The gnomon cast a shadow on the dial. As the Sun moved across the sky, the shadow moved across lines on the dial. Each line stood for a certain time of day.

Around 300 B.C., a Babylonian astronomer named Berosus made a sundial with a curved base. It looked sort of like a bowl. The gnomon stood in the center of the bowl. Lines on the base of the bowl divided the day into twelve equal parts. These were the first hours. Berosus's clock was so good that others like it were used for more than a thousand years. Our modern system of twenty-four-hour days, with twelve hours in the morning and twelve hours in the afternoon and evening, began with Berosus's system.

COUNTING BY 60s

Three pencils, three cars, and three stars in the sky all have something in common: "threeness." Ten birds and ten trees share the trait of being ten in number. By understanding this connection, people in the ancient Middle East were able to create symbols for numbers. Then they could describe any group of three objects with a certain symbol. A different symbol could stand for a collection of two, four, and so on. Archaeologists have found clay tablets marked with numbers in the ruins of Babylon and other ancient Middle Eastern cities. These are

▶ A clay tablet from the Sumerian city of Ur records numbers of laborers in 2000 B.C.

BABYLONIANS AND ZERO

The Babylonians were advanced in developing their place-value system. They were also pioneers in using a symbol to stand for zero: 0. A dot stood for 0 in their numbering system. However, they used 0 merely as a placeholder in numbers and not as a number itself. It would be as if we used 0 to show the difference between 44 and 404, but never used 0 on its own.

some of the world's earliest known number symbols. Some tablets are nearly five thousand years old.

The Mesopotamian numbering system was based on 60. Symbols on the tablets stood for 1 through 59. The symbol for 1 also stood for 60 or 3,600 (60 × 60), depending on its place in a number. Sound confusing? It's not really. In the same way, we can use a 1 to stand for 100, as in the number 156. This kind of number system is called a place-value system.

LUNAR ECLIPSES

During an eclipse of the Moon, Earth passes between the Sun and the Moon. Earth's shadow darkens the Moon. To ancient peoples, eclipses were mysterious and frightening.

Babylonian astronomers wanted to know when eclipses would occur. They watched the Sun and other bright objects move through the sky.

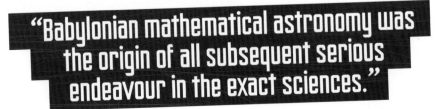

"Babylonian mathematical astronomy was the origin of all subsequent serious endeavour in the exact sciences."

— Asger Aaboe, Danish historian, 1974

For centuries the astronomers recorded the dates of eclipses and the movements of heavenly bodies. They used a calendar based on the phases of the Moon.

Ancient scientists did not understand why eclipses occurred. But they learned when to expect them—every 223 months (by our modern calendar). Their work was the start of what we call mathematical astronomy.

A FAMOUS NUMBER

One of the most useful numbers to engineers, physicists, and other scientists is pi. Multiplying pi by the diameter of a circle (the distance across the middle) gives you the circle's circumference (distance around the outside).

PI: WHAT WE'VE LEARNED SINCE ANCIENT TIMES

As far as mathematicians know, pi is not equal to any exact fraction or decimal number. It is slightly less than 22 ÷ 7. Mathematicians have used modern computers to figure pi's value to nearly 3 trillion decimal places—that's 3, then a decimal point followed by 3 trillion numbers. But the decimals that ancient mathematicians used were close enough for their purposes.

The ancient Babylonians and Egyptians discovered pi around 2000 B.C. They found the number by studying how the circumference of a circle changes as its diameter changes. Babylonian mathematicians figured that pi was equal to 3.125. Egyptians figured the number at 3.160. Modern mathematicians define pi as approximately 3.1416.

Pi was one of the greatest discoveries in computing history. Pi works on each and every circle, no matter what the size. Ancient people could compute the distance around any circular field, building, or other object by measuring the circle's diameter and multiplying by about 3.1.

CHAPTER THREE

ANCIENT EGYPT

▲ The ancient Egyptians settled along the Nile River *(above)*. They developed hieroglyphic writing and numbers as a way to record history, to keep track of business, and to execute construction projects, among other things.

People in ancient Egypt began to settle along the Nile River around 7000 B.C. The Nile provided water for drinking, bathing, and growing crops. The river also overflowed its banks every year. When it did, it deposited a layer of muck that fertilized the soil. Gradually, the Egyptians developed one of the ancient world's most famous civilizations. The ancient Egyptians built giant pyramids, devised a picture-writing system called hieroglyphics, and created other advanced technology.

The ancient Egyptians used computing technology for many projects. They used addition and subtraction to keep track of taxes and business deals. They used surveying to measure farmers' fields. They measured time with sundials and other types of clocks. They used engineering techniques such as measuring right angles (angles that are perpendicular, measuring 90 degrees) to build giant pyramids and temples.

PICTURE NUMBERS

Mention hieroglyphics, and most people think of the Egyptian system of picture writing. But hieroglyphics was also picture numbering. In the Egyptian system, a single line stood for 1, two lines for 2, three lines for 3, and so on up to 9. An archlike symbol stood for 10. A spiral represented 100. The number 1,000 was represented by a lotus plant. A picture of an index finger meant 10,000. The picture for 100,000 was a tadpole or a frog. A man sitting with arms upraised stood for 1,000,000.

To write the number 1,109, an Egyptian scribe would draw a lotus plant (1,000), a spiral (100), and nine lines (9). One finger, one lotus, and two spirals meant 11,200. A man and a tadpole together stood for 1,100,000.

▲ The White Chapel, built in the 1900s B.C., contains records of each Egyptian nome (ancient district) and its measurements. The records are carved in the white alabaster stone walls of the chapel (above).

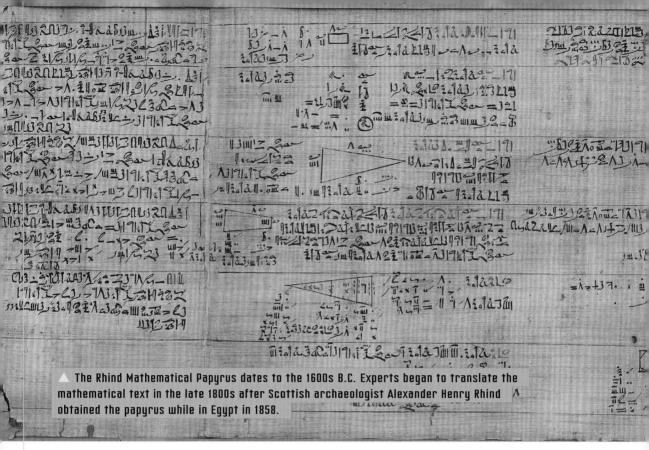

ANCIENT TEXTBOOKS

In the 1800s, archaeologists discovered two textbooks used in schools in ancient Egypt. Both books were long scrolls of papyrus, a kind of paper made from the papyrus plant. The books had been used to teach scribes. These professionals were trained to read, write, and perform equations in ancient times.

The Rhind Mathematical Papyrus is our most important source of information about Egyptian math. It was named for Alexander Henry Rhind, a Scottish archaeologist. He obtained the scroll near the Egyptian city of Thebes in 1858. The scroll is about 18 feet (5.5 meters) long when it's unrolled.

An Egyptian scribe, Ahmes the Moonborn, wrote the papyrus around 1650 B.C. He called it "insight into all that exists, knowledge of all secrets." The papyrus explained how to add, subtract, and do other computations with whole numbers and fractions. Most ancient Egyptians were not educated.

They wouldn't have understood the scroll, which explains why its contents were considered "secrets." But the equations would be a snap for most modern sixth-grade students.

Ahmes also included more advanced math in his textbook, including algebra. This branch of math uses symbols to stand for numbers. One simple algebra equation is $6 + x = 7$. The answer is $x = 1$. Another algebra equation is $45 - x = 40$. The answer: $x = 5$.

The Egyptians used algebra to solve practical problems. For instance, suppose one thousand stonecutters were building a pyramid. Each stonecutter ate three loaves of bread a day. How much bread would be needed to feed the stonecutters for ten days? The equation: $x = 1,000 \times 3 \times 10$.

The Rhind Papyrus also included brainteasers and word problems. See if you can solve the following one, just as Egyptian students had to.

Seven houses contain seven cats. Each cat kills seven mice. Each mouse had eaten seven ears of grain. Each ear of grain would have produced seven measures of wheat. What is the total of all these items together? *See the answer below.*

FRACTIONS, THE EGYPTIAN WAY

Egyptians used fractions to multiply and divide. They mainly used unit fractions—fractions with a 1 on top—such as $\frac{1}{2}$ or $\frac{1}{4}$. In modern times, students often learn to work with fractions by making both *bottom* numbers match up, no matter what's on top. Most people consider this method easier than working with unit fractions. So maybe you should be glad you're not an Egyptian math student!

ANSWER: 19,607 items

The Moscow Mathematical Papyrus, another ancient Egyptian scroll, was used in the 1800s B.C. It is named for the Russian city where it's kept. The scroll is sometimes called the Golenishchev Papyrus, after the man who bought it in Egypt in the 1890s. The author of the ancient scroll is unknown.

Like the Rhind Papyrus, the Moscow Papyrus included practical arithmetic and algebra problems. Some problems calculated the rate at which a worker could do a job. Others found a ship's measurements. The Moscow Papyrus also involved geometry. For one problem, students had to find the volume of a pyramid with its top missing. Another example involved finding surface area.

STRANGE MULTIPLYING AND DIVIDING

The ancient Egyptian civilization spanned several thousand years. Egyptian computing methods changed over that time. One way the Egyptians multiplied numbers may seem quite strange to modern students. In the Old Kingdom period (about 2650 to 2150 B.C.), Egyptians used two columns of numbers. The left column always began with 1 and doubled with each row. The right column began with the number to be multiplied and doubled with each row. Suppose a student wanted to multiply 30 by 12. The student first made two columns:

1	30
2	60
4	120
8	240
16	480

The student would then write down numbers from the first column that added up to 12: 4 + 8 = 12. Then the student would add the "partners" of those numbers from the next column to get the answer: 120 + 240 = 360.

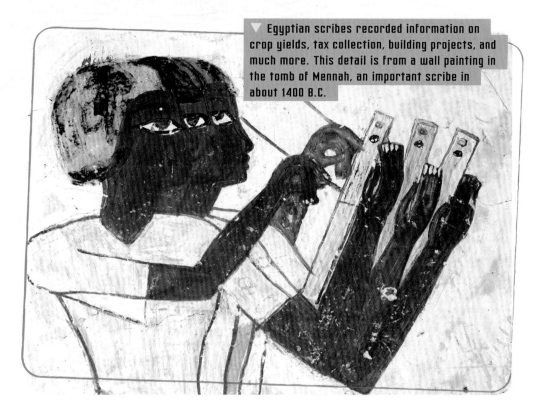

Egyptian scribes recorded information on crop yields, tax collection, building projects, and much more. This detail is from a wall painting in the tomb of Mennah, an important scribe in about 1400 B.C.

HOW MUCH IS ENOUGH?

In ancient Egypt, scribes were important people. They kept records, figured taxes, managed building projects, and helped the military determine how much food and equipment it needed.

The Rhind and Moscow papyruses explained how to solve the kinds of problems that scribes would encounter in their work. The books had lessons on measuring the area of fields, adding up numbers of bricks, and calculating the amount of bread and beer needed to feed construction workers.

MEASURING WITH KNOTS

The Egyptians used simple methods for measuring the size of fields and buildings. Sometimes they used wooden rods of standard lengths, like modern yardsticks or metersticks, to measure distances. Other times, they used long,

knotted ropes. They tied knots an equal distance, such as one cubit, from one another. They ran the rope along the ground or against the side of a building. The Egyptians then counted the knots to determine the length.

A drawing on a tomb built at Thebes around 1400 B.C. shows people using a knotted rope to measure a field of grain. One man holds each end of the rope, which is stretched along the side of the field. Meanwhile, two other men record the measurement. The men look much like officials at modern football games using a 10-yard (9 m) chain to measure the football's advance.

GREAT SURVEYORS

It took great surveyors to build the Great Pyramid at Giza, completed around 2560 B.C. The pyramid was 481 feet (147 m) high and was built from more than two million stone blocks. (Due to erosion, or wearing away, it is about 30 feet (9 m) shorter in modern times.) Its base is 755 feet (230 m) long on each side and covers an area nearly the size of ten football fields. Yet the sides of the base come within 7 inches (18 cm) of forming a perfect square. They are pointed almost exactly in north-south and east-west directions.

How did Egyptian surveyors work so accurately? Part of their secret was a tool called the *groma*. They used it to make right angles. The groma was a flat wooden cross. Its arms intersected in the middle to form four right angles. At both ends of each arm, cords were attached. Weights were tied to the cords. The weighted cords hung straight down, forming more right angles with the arms of the cross. Ancient surveyors lined up the groma's arms and cords with

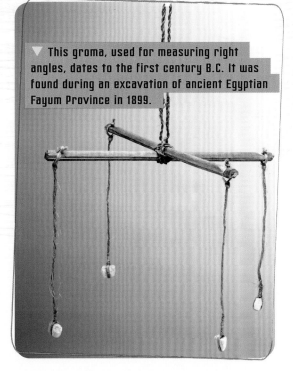

▼ This groma, used for measuring right angles, dates to the first century B.C. It was found during an excavation of ancient Egyptian Fayum Province in 1899.

the walls and ceilings of buildings. Gromas helped builders make sure that the walls formed perfect right angles with one another.

THE NILOMETER

The Nile's yearly flooding was important to Egyptian farmers. Too little flooding meant less water for crops and a bad harvest. Too much flooding could damage farms and cities. Around 3000 B.C., the Egyptians created a device for computing the Nile's flood. Archaeologists call it the Nilometer. Nilometers were stone pillars or steps along the riverbanks, marked with measurements. They measured the water level when the Nile overflowed.

Scribes and priests kept records of the floods for centuries. Year after year, they compared water levels to crop production. Scribes concluded that a flood of about 16 cubits—27 feet, or 8 meters—was best for the important crops of wheat and barley.

Visitors to Cairo, Egypt, can tour the Nilometer on Roda Island. As the Nile's water level rises, marks on the wooden post measure its height. Most of the structure that was built in A.D. 715 was destroyed by floodwaters many times. The existing nilometer was rebuilt in 1092.

ANCIENT TAX REFORM

According to the ancient Greek historian Herodotus, geometry was invented for tax purposes! Geometry is a form of math used to find the area of squares, rectangles, and other figures. In the fifth century B.C., Herodotus wrote about Sesostris, an Egyptian pharaoh (king) from about 1400 B.C. Sesostris charged his subjects a tax based on the amount of land that each person farmed. But every year when the Nile flooded, soil washed into the river. Some farmers lost big pieces of land. So the pharaoh ruled that farmers who had lost land could pay lower taxes. Scribes measured the amount of land that had been lost. Herodotus reasoned, "From this practice, I think, geometry first came to be known in Egypt, whence it passed into Greece."

Herodotus may have a good story, but historians don't trust it. Some of the names, dates, and facts that Herodotus used in his writings were simply wrong. And experts know that no pharaoh named Sesostris ruled around 1400 B.C. None of the pharaohs from that time perfectly match the pharaoh in Herodotus's stories, either. Whether or not the story is true, it demonstrates just how useful surveying and computing were in ancient Egyptian society.

> **"For the Egyptians had to perform [land] measurements because the overflow of the Nile would cause the boundary of each person's land to disappear. . . . The discovery both of [geometry] and of the other sciences proceeded from utility."**

—Proclus Diadochus, Greek philosopher, A.D. 410–485

THE GRAIN

The smallest official unit of weight in the United States and the United Kingdom is the grain. A grain is tiny. It takes 437.5 grains to equal 1 ounce (28 grams) and 7,000 grains to equal 1 pound (0.45 kilograms).

The ancient Egyptians first used this unit of measurement thousands of years ago. It originally equaled the weight of one grain of wheat. Merchants selling small amounts of precious goods, such as gold, would put several grains of wheat on one side of a beam scale. They weighed out the goods on the other side.

▼ In the tomb of Mereruka, a powerful Egyptian official who lived around 2200 B.C., a relief carving depicts men weighing items on a beam scale.

SHADOW CLOCKS, SUNDIALS, AND WATER CLOCKS

Timekeeping was important to people in ancient Egypt. Priests and soldiers had to perform certain tasks at certain times. Rulers, government officials, and scribes had to keep track of workers and their time on the job.

Like the Babylonians, the Egyptians divided daylight into twelve equal parts. The Egyptians used clocks as early as 3500 B.C. The first Egyptian clock was an obelisk, a tall, four-sided pillar. It cast a shadow as the Sun moved past. The shadow grew shorter throughout the morning as the Sun rose in the sky. It disappeared at noon with the Sun directly overhead. The shadow lengthened throughout the afternoon as the Sun dipped in the western sky. People estimated the time based on the length of the shadow.

Sometime around 1500 B.C., the Egyptians made a new and improved sundial. It looked like the letter *T* stuck in the ground. A long, narrow base extended behind it along the ground. Lines on the base marked the hours. Egyptians could tell the time of day by looking at which line the bar's shadow reached. Later, they used sundials in the shape of half circles, like those used in the ancient Middle East. As the Sun moved through the sky, a gnomon cast a shadow on lines spreading out from the center. These early sundials marked twelve hours of daylight year-round. But in Egypt, as in most places, the amount of daylight changes with the seasons. So the length of hours actually varied. With this technology, an hour wasn't a standardized measure of time. Each hour was longer in the summer and shorter in the winter.

Also around 1500 B.C., the Egyptians built another kind of timekeeper. It was the clepsydra, or water clock. It was made of a clay jar with markings on the inside. Unlike sundials, water clocks could keep time at night. As water in the jar dribbled out of a small hole at the bottom, more and more markings were exposed. Each mark that showed meant that another unit of time had passed. Clepsydras had to be made very precisely so they all kept time the same. Water had to flow out of each one at about the same rate.

> This replica of an ancient Egyptian water clock is based on the original version carved from alabaster stone. There are ten columns of twelve indentations around the inside of the clock. As water drained from a hole in the bottom at a regular rate, more indentations became visible. People could tell how much time had passed.

SUMMER IN DECEMBER?

The solar year is the time Earth takes to travel around the Sun. It takes approximately 365 days, five hours, forty-eight minutes, and forty-six seconds. What would happen if the calendar didn't match the solar year? Holidays and seasons would gradually shift. Summer months would eventually fall in the middle of winter.

The first ancient calendars did shift in this way. They were created according to the lunar year. The lunar year is divided into twelve months based on the phases of the Moon. It lasts only 354 days. Because of the difference between the lunar year and the solar year, the first calendars were not very accurate. They shifted 110 days—almost four months—every ten years.

The Egyptians were the first people to solve the problem. They created a calendar based on the solar year. The Egyptian calendar had twelve months of thirty days each, with five extra days added at the end of each year. In 238 B.C., the pharaoh Ptolemy III made the calendar even more accurate. He added an extra day every fourth year. That day made up for the nearly six-hour difference (about one-quarter of a day) between the calendar year and the solar year. A year with an extra day is a leap year.

CHAPTER FOUR

ANCIENT INDIA

Mohenjo-daro, built around 2600 B.C., was one of the largest settlements of the Indus Valley Civilization. The ruins, discovered in 1922, are located in modern-day Pakistan.

People in modern-day Pakistan, Afghanistan, and the northwestern part of India began settling into villages around 4000 B.C. During the next thousand years, a thriving society developed there. We call it the Indus Valley Civilization because it developed along the Indus River valley.

Historians were unaware of the Indus Valley Civilization until the 1920s. Then archaeologists found remains of ancient brick buildings and began to explore the area. They discovered the city of Harappa in 1921 and Mohenjo-daro in 1922. Eventually, archaeologists uncovered remains of hundreds of cities and towns.

Evidence shows that the Indus Valley Civilization lasted from 2500 to 1500 B.C. We still do not know why the civilization collapsed. But we do know that the ancient Indians introduced several advances in computing technology. Later groups of people in India also made important developments in computing.

ARABIC NUMERALS = INDIAN NUMERALS

The credit for major technological advances sometimes gets lost in history. That certainly is the case with the numerals used in most of the modern world. We usually call them Arabic numerals—but ancient Indian people actually developed them.

The ancient Indian numbering system allows people to write down any number, no matter how big, with just 10

symbols: 0, 1, 2, 3, 4, 5, 6, 7, 8, and 9. The first known versions of a few numerals in this system appear on pillars built by Ashoka, an Indian king, around 250 B.C. Then in the first century A.D., early versions of the numerals 1 through 9 appeared. These early numerals have been found on cave walls near Nasik, India. The numeral 0 probably came into use around A.D. 600.

◄ The pillars of Ashoka were built in the 200s B.C., during the reign of King Ashoka. They stood up to 50 feet (15 m) high in locations throughout northern India, Nepal, and Pakistan. Some inscriptions include early versions of modern numerals. Only fragments of the original pillars *(such as the one at left)* still exist.

THE CHANGING SHAPES OF HINDU-ARABIC NUMERALS

The Hindu-Arabic numerals we use in modern times came from ancient Indian symbols. But these first-century symbols for 1 through 9 looked quite different. They were part of the Brahmi script. The symbols for 1, 2, and 3 were simply horizontal lines. The symbols for 6 and 7 looked similar to their modern forms at first. But they changed over time. By the 900s, 1 was a vertical line instead of a horizontal line. Scribes had connected the lines in the numerals 2 and 3. So these looked much like the modern symbols. This shortcut let scribes avoid lifting their writing tools off the page. Other symbols had changed in various ways. And by this time, the symbol for 0 was in use.

By about 1100, knowledge of the Indian numbering system had spread. People in other parts of Asia and northern Africa began using the numerals. Different versions of the symbols evolved in each region. Sometimes symbols were rotated from earlier versions. Some numerals changed through many small differences, such as the tilt or the length of a line.

In eastern Africa and the Middle East, the numerals eventually became the numerals in modern Arabic. In other parts of Asia, the symbols took on their modern forms in the Tibetan, Thai, and Vietnamese scripts. The Indian symbols slowly changed in northern Africa and Spain too. By about 1500, they became the modern numerals that we recognize as 0 through 9.

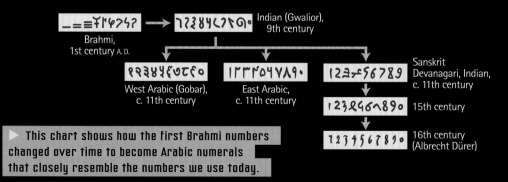

This chart shows how the first Brahmi numbers changed over time to become Arabic numerals that closely resemble the numbers we use today.

Middle Easterners learned about the numbers by trading with India. They adapted the system for their own use. By A.D. 976, Europeans had learned the system from the Middle East. Europeans didn't know about the numerals' roots in ancient India, so they named them Arabic numerals (named for Arabs, a people of the Middle East). But modern mathematicians acknowledge the system's Hindu, or Indian, origin. Since the 1920s, the number system has also been known as Hindu-Arabic.

THE POWER OF ZERO

People in India began using a decimal system around the A.D. 500s. A decimal system is based on multiples of ten. The number system used in the United States and most other countries is a decimal system. Within a century or two, 0 also appeared in the Indian system of mathematics. An Indian temple built in 876 holds the first known written 0 used as a number, not just a placeholder. This was an important advance in computing. The 0 is necessary to the place-value system, which enables numbers to hold different values,

"It is India that gave us the ingenious method of expressing all numbers by means of ten symbols, each symbol receiving a value of position as well as an absolute value; . . . and we shall appreciate the grandeur of this achievement the more when we remember that it escaped the genius of [Greek mathematicians] Archimedes and Apollonius, two of the greatest men produced by antiquity."

—Pierre-Simon Laplace (1749–1827), French mathematician

depending on their placement. Think about the number 220. Each 2 has a different value, depending on its position in the number. The first 2 stands for 200. The second stands for 20. If a 0 weren't on the right, the number would look like 22.

The place-value system with 0 made adding, subtracting, multiplying, and dividing easy. Numbers could be written one under another in columns and lined up according to value. Adding and subtracting became a snap. (Just try adding or subtracting large numbers with Egyptian hieroglyphics to see how hard it is without the place-value system.)

MATH AND RELIGION

The Hindu religion, first practiced in ancient India, played a big role in encouraging advanced mathematics. As early as three thousand years ago, altars for ritual had to be built in precise shapes and sizes. Parts of the Vedas, sacred books of Hinduism, described the rules for building altars. One altar might have to be circular and measure a certain area. The next altar might have to be a square equal in area to the circular altar. The sacred texts gave formulas for these constructions.

▼ An Indian man reads from the Vedas, a set of four ancient Hindu religious texts written between 1500 and 500 B.C. Parts of the Vedas describe shapes and sizes of altars based on mathematical principles.

Why did the altars have these requirements for their size and shape? A main theme of the sacred Hindu texts was connecting the heavens, Earth, and the living. The altars were a crucial part of making these connections. Three shapes of altars stood for Earth, atmosphere, or space. Together the altars represented the universe. The numbers of stones or bricks used to build them were related to the length of the lunar and solar years.

Through the Vedas and the rules for altar construction, historians have realized how much ancient Indians knew about astronomy. In fact, other measurements within Indian temples represented the distances of the Sun and the Moon from Earth.

FATHER OF SINE

The term *trigonometry* comes from Greek words that mean "the measurement of triangles." Six functions, or ratios, are at the heart of this branch of mathematics. They are used to determine the sizes of the sides and angles of triangles. One of these six functions is called sine.

An ancient Hindu mathematician, Aryabhata the Elder, computed the first sine tables. These lists showed the value of sine for angles of many sizes. The tables let mathematicians do trigonometry quickly, without stopping to figure out the sine for each angle. Aryabhata included the tables in his book *Aryabhatiyam*, written in A.D. 499.

In addition to trigonometry, the book included formulas and rules for algebra, geometry, and arithmetic. It included one the most accurate values of pi that had been found to that time, 3.1416. Aryabhata also introduced a way to find the length of a side of a cube with a known volume. We call this a cube root.

CHAPTER FIVE

ANCIENT CHINA

The ancient Chinese were advanced mathematicians. They developed the basis for a decimal system and invented the first automated computing device, the abacus. They may have even discovered ideas of geometry before the Greeks made those ideas famous.

STICK NUMBERS AND COUNTING BOARDS

The Chinese wrote different kinds of numerals over time. As early as 1500 B.C., ancient priests carved one type of numerals into shells and bones. They used these objects in ceremonies to gain insight to the future. The inscriptions recorded the number of animals sacrificed, prisoners taken in war, animals hunted, and more. These are the earliest recorded Chinese numerals. Lines and curves formed the symbols for the numbers 1 through 9. These combined with symbols for 10, 100, and 1,000 to make larger numbers.

Beginning around 400 B.C., stick numerals were used in a place-value system. These numerals were short lines. The numbers 1 to 5 were represented with one to five lines. T-shaped figures were used to show

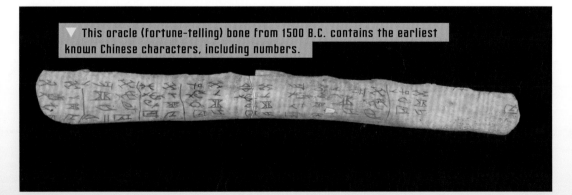

▼ This oracle (fortune-telling) bone from 1500 B.C. contains the earliest known Chinese characters, including numbers.

the numbers 6 to 9. The numeral on the right stood for the ones, the next numeral to the left stood for the tens, the next for hundreds, and so on.

Stick numerals likely got their start with counting rods. Math students and scholars in ancient China did calculations with rods on counting boards. The boards were made from wood and were separated into columns or squares. People used sets of red and black counting rods for positive and negative numbers. Each counting rod was about 4 inches (10 cm) long. A full set contained 271 sticks.

Rods were placed on the counting board's squares, with each column from right to left representing the 1s, 10s, 100s, 1,000s, and so forth. Rods that were not carefully placed on the board could cause confusion. So by the A.D. 200s, stick numbers used lines in alternating directions. The 1s numeral, on the right, used vertical lines. The 10s column used horizontal lines, then vertical lines for the 100s, and the pattern repeated. An empty square stood for 0. Sometime after A.D. 700, when people in India began using a symbol for 0, use of the symbol passed into China also.

▼ The Chinese used stick numerals in a place-value system. Vertical numerals represented 1 through 9. Horizontal numerals in the next column stood for 10, 20, 30, and so on. The hundreds, in another column, were vertical again. Alternating directions of the numerals allowed the Chinese to write them close together without mixing up columns.

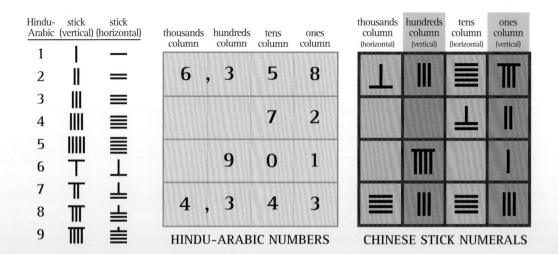

HINDU-ARABIC NUMBERS   CHINESE STICK NUMERALS

NINE CHAPTERS

The *Jiuzhang suanshu*, or *Nine Chapters on Mathematical Procedures*, is the most famous ancient Chinese mathematical text. It dates from between 200 B.C. and A.D. 50. This ancient work contains 246 math problems. It was a required textbook for math students from the seventh through the twelfth centuries A.D.

The problems in the *Nine Chapters* show the variety of math skills that the Chinese valued. The first set of math problems involve surveying. Another set required students to find proportions and percentages for trading goods. Other sets of problems involved questions of engineering, taxes, and finding costs. Many of the problems in the *Nine Chapters* required complicated calculations with fractions.

ASTRONOMY IN ANCIENT TEXTS

Like other ancient cultures, the ancient Chinese took an interest in the movement of the Sun, the Moon, the stars, and other heavenly objects. They carefully kept track of changes in the night sky. Chinese records of lunar and solar eclipses date back to the 1200s B.C. Those are some of the oldest eclipse records in existence.

Astronomy is the focus of one famous Chinese text. The *Zhoubi Suanjing* is one of China's

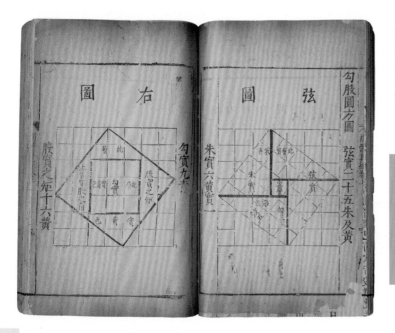

◀ Pages from *Zhoubi Suanjing*, written between 100 B.C. and A.D. 100, illustrate the Pythagorean Theorem of triangles. This copy of the book was reprinted from the Chinese original in 1603.

CALCULATING PI

Several Chinese mathematicians found impressively accurate values of pi. In A.D. 264, Liu Hui used a polygon (a closed shape with any number of straight edges, or sides) to mimic the shape of a large circle. His polygon had 3,072 sides. He knew how to find the perimeter and radius of that shape, so he could then solve for pi. He found that pi = 3.14159. The true value of pi has endless decimals, but when rounded to five decimal places, this value is exactly right.

A father-son team of mathematicians sought an even more precise value in about 480. Tsu Ch'ung-Chih and Tsu Keng-Chih found the value of pi to be about 355 ÷ 113. That's 3.1415929203 when rounded to ten decimal places. It remained the most accurate value of pi for about 1,200 years.

"ten mathematical classics," along with the *Nine Chapters*. The text was put together between 100 B.C. and A.D. 100, though its material is believed to be older. Much of the work focuses on measuring the positions and movements of objects in the sky with a gnomon. Its title means "Zhou Shadow Gauge Manual."

Another part of the manual discusses side lengths and areas of right triangles. For many years, this text has been credited with proving how the lengths of the sides of a right triangle are related. In geometry this formula is known as the Pythagorean theorem. (A theorem is a statement that has been proved or is to be proved.) It is named for the ancient Greek philosopher Pythagoras. But the material of this book is thought to be older than Pythagoras. Was the Pythagorean theorem actually a Chinese discovery? Modern scholars aren't sure. It's possible that the text was misinterpreted by translators or other mathematicians who added comments over time.

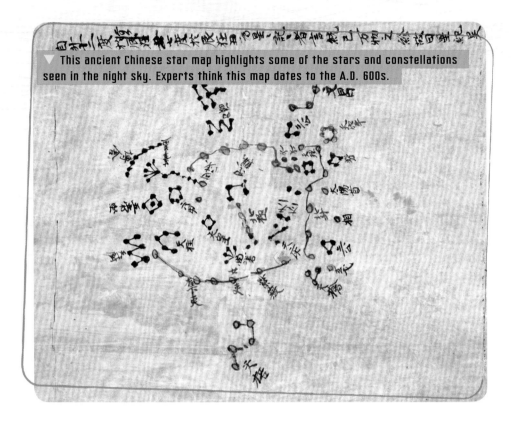

This ancient Chinese star map highlights some of the stars and constellations seen in the night sky. Experts think this map dates to the A.D. 600s.

THE FIRST STAR CHARTS

Astronomers in ancient China created the earliest known star charts. One of these charts was discovered in the early 1900s. It lay among thousands of ancient documents in a cave in Dunhuang, in northern China. The chart is 6.5 feet (2 m) long, and it shows 1,339 stars in red, black, and white ink. The famous shapes of the Big Dipper and Orion are easily picked out.

In 1959 experts examined the chart and determined that it dated to about A.D. 940. However, in 2009 experts at the British Library in the United Kingdom reexamined the ancient map before putting it on display. They realized it was made hundreds of years earlier than thought, probably between 649 and 684. That makes it the world's earliest known scientific map of the sky. In fact, because of the type of paper used and the lack of any calculations, experts believe the chart is a copy of an even older work.

THE CHINESE CALENDAR

Many ancient calendars were often based on either the solar year or the lunar year. Since the Chinese were such careful astronomers, they wanted their calendar to closely match the cycles of both the Sun and the Moon. From the fourteenth century B.C., the Chinese calendar used lunar months of twenty-nine or thirty days. An extra month was added when needed to help the calendar align with the solar year. How did they know when to add an extra month? They tracked the angle of the Sun precisely through the year. They could tell when months were too far ahead of the Sun's position in the sky. When that happened, they simply repeated one month. This happens about once every three years.

This calendar is still used to determine the Chinese New Year and other festival dates. However, in daily life, China generally uses the same calendar that's used in most other countries.

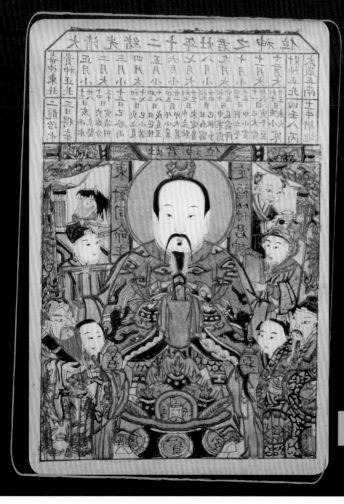

◄ A Chinese lunar calendar from 1895

ANCIENT COMPUTERS

The Chinese developed one of the world's most lasting computing devices—the abacus. Early forms of the abacus appeared during the Chou dynasty (the period when the Chou family ruled), from about 1122 to 256 B.C. But a later version proved more useful, making the abacus a more common tool. It was in widespread use in China by about A.D. 1200. In fact, it is still a popular calculating tool in some parts of Asia.

The abacus could be considered the world's first computer. It was used for addition, subtraction, multiplication, and division. With the abacus, people could perform these calculations much faster than they could with counting boards or numbers written on paper.

The abacus consisted of a rectangular frame divided into two parts. Beads slid up and down along a series of vertical rods in each part. Computing with an abacus was simple. With the device flat on a table, the user moved and counted the beads. A bead was "counted" when it was moved toward the crossbar separating the decks. The upper deck had two beads on each rod. Each of those beads had a value of 5. The lower deck had five beads on each rod. Those beads each had a value of 1.

"Of all the ancient calculating instruments, the Chinese abacus is the only one to provide a simple means to carry out all the operations of arithmetic; Western [U.S. and European] observers are usually astonished at the speed and [ease] with which even the most complicated arithmetic can be done."

—Georges Ifrah, French math historian, 2001

▲ A Chinese abacus uses five beads per rod on the lower deck and two per rod on the upper deck. Abacuses in other countries used different combinations, such as four and one, or ten beads per rod with no divider.

Each vertical rod represented a place value—the 1s, 10s, 100s, 1,000s, and so on. To show the number 4,321 on an abacus, the user moved one bead on the lower right rod toward the crossbar, two beads on the next rod over, three on the third rod, and four on the next.

When five beads on a rod had been counted, the user "carried" the number to the upper deck, moving one of the upper beads to the crossbar and all five lower beads away from it. When both upper beads on a rod had been counted, the user carried the number to the next rod to the left by moving one of the lower beads toward the crossbar.

CHAPTER SIX

THE ANCIENT AMERICAS

The ancient Maya built the city of Tikal in Guatemala in around A.D. 200. It remained a center of religion and politics for the Maya into the A.D. 900s.

While ancient cultures in Europe, Africa, and Asia thrived, so did groups in North America and South America. For thousands of years, civilizations and empires in the ancient Americas rose and fell. They couldn't share information with other groups across the oceans. So they created their own systems. Several ancient American groups made significant advances in computing technology—without any knowledge of the discoveries made halfway around the world.

The Maya, based in modern-day Mexico and Central America, began settling into farming villages before 1200 B.C. Eventually, Mayan towns and cities stretched from southern Mexico through the modern-day countries of Honduras, Guatemala, El Salvador, and Belize. The culture thrived from about A.D. 200 to 900.

Mayan computing technology included a numeral system, mathematics, and an accurate calendar. Mayan computing was more advanced, in some ways, than math used at the same time in Europe, Asia, and Africa. Specifically, Mayan mathematics included the concept of zero, which was not widely used in other parts of the world until later.

COUNTING BY 20s

Most modern societies use a decimal system, based on the number 10. Place values increase in powers of 10: 1, 10, 100, 1,000, 10,000, 100,000, 1,000,000, and so on. The Maya, however, used a system based on the number 20. (This is called a vigesimal system, from the Latin for "twentieth.") In the Mayan system, place values increased in powers of 20: 1, 20, 400, 8,000, 160,000. To build the number 62, the Maya used three 20s and two 1s, instead of six 10s and two 1s as modern Americans do. We don't know why the Maya used the base-20 system—perhaps because people have twenty fingers and toes in all.

▼ This page from the Dresden Codex shows many Maya numerals. The Dresden Codex, written in around the 1100s, is a compilation of earlier Maya almanacs and astrological and religious information.

Mayan numerals consisted of dots and bars. One dot stood for 1, and two dots stood for 2. One bar stood for 5, and two bars stood for 10. The Maya combined dots and bars to write larger numbers. One bar and four dots, for instance, stood for 9. Two bars and two dots stood for 12.

ZERO PIONEERS

The ancient Maya were one of the earliest peoples to use a symbol for zero as a placeholder. They probably used it by the A.D. 300s—long before most civilizations used such a symbol. Their base-20 number system, which included zero, came into use in the several centuries that followed. The Mayan symbol for zero was a small oval with several lines inside.

The Mayan zero was first merely a placeholder, for example to distinguish 26 from 206. But it was used as a number later on in Mayan culture, still hundreds of years before Europeans caught on to its use.

NUMBERS ALL IN A ROW

The Mayan numbering system depended on position, just like our modern place-value system. Our numbers increase in value from right to left, with 1s in the right-hand position, 10s in the next spot, then 100s, and so on. But in the Mayan system, numerals were written from bottom to top. And because the Maya used a base-20 system, values increased in powers of 20: 1s on the bottom row, 20s above them, 400s next, and so on.

HOLY NUMBERS

The Maya believed that some numbers were holy, including 20, the basis for the Mayan numbering system. The number 5 was also special, maybe because people have five fingers on each hand. The Mayan century had fifty-two years, so the number 52 was holy. The number 400 was very special—it was the number of gods of the night. The number 13 was special because the Maya thought that the sky consisted of thirteen layers.

THE MAYAN CALENDAR

In Mayan culture, some days were lucky—and some unlucky. Lucky days were chosen for important activities such as weddings, battles, and planting

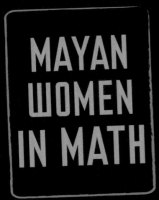

MAYAN WOMEN IN MATH

Mathematicians held an honored spot in Mayan society. They helped keep the calendar, and they predicted the movements of celestial bodies. Mathematicians also made business calculations, computing prices of goods and land, for instance.

Mathematicians were shown in Mayan picture writing by a special symbol that included a scroll with numbers. The first mathematician identified in Mayan picture writing was a woman. We don't know her name or anything about her. But she must have been very important.

and harvesting crops. The Maya also celebrated many religious holidays, which had to be observed on the same days each year. To keep track of lucky days and holidays, the Maya needed an accurate calendar—one in step with the solar year.

The Maya used two calendars. The Tzolkin, or sacred calendar, contained 260 days. The days were named after Mayan gods, thought to carry time across the sky. The Tzolkin was used in combination with the Haab, a 365-day calendar based on the solar year.

The Mayan calendars were complicated. They were based on movements of the Sun, the Moon, and the planet Venus. Historians do not know exactly how the Mayan calendars were developed, but they came into use in the first century A.D. Their solar calendar was more accurate than any other calendar in the ancient world.

The Maya also kept track of passing days with a third system, the Long Count. The Maya had calculated what they considered to be the date the world was created—August 11, 3113 B.C., by our modern calendar. The Long Count recorded the number of days since that date. Mayan

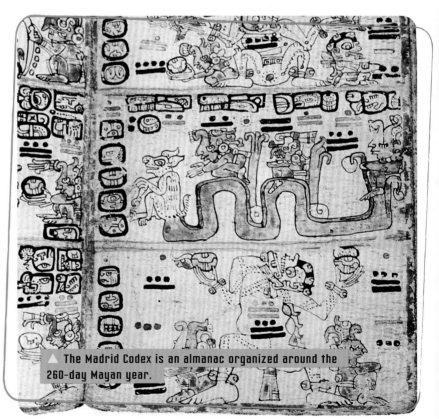

▲ The Madrid Codex is an almanac organized around the 260-day Mayan year.

> "The Mayan concern for understanding the cycles of celestial bodies, particularly the Sun, the Moon and Venus, led them to accumulate a large set of highly accurate observations."

—Luis F. Rodríguez, astronomer, 1985

numbers show the Long Count date on Stela 29, a stone monument found in the ancient city of Tikal, Guatemala. It dates from A.D. 292. The Long Count date appears as 8.12.14.8.15—meaning 1,243,615 days since the Mayan creation.

THE AZTEC CALENDAR

Several hundred years after the Mayan civilization had dwindled, the Aztec Empire became a powerful force in Mexico and Central America. Between the early 1300s and 1500s, this group ruled land from central Mexico to Guatemala, El Salvador, and Honduras. The city of Tenochtitlán, at the site of modern Mexico City, was the heart of the empire.

The Aztec calendar was similar to the Mayan calendars. Like the Maya, the Aztecs measured time in three different ways. A 260-day sacred calendar kept track of which Aztec gods ruled over the days and weeks. This was the *tonalpohualli*. A 365-day calendar, the *xiupohualli*, measured the solar year. It kept track of seasons. The start of these two calendars matched up just once every fifty-two years. This stretch of 18,980 days, or fifty-two years, made up the third Aztec calendar.

In 1790 workers making repairs on the central square in Mexico City unearthed a huge, sculpted circular stone known as the Sun Stone. They found it among the ruins of Tenochtitlán beneath the modern city. People often call it a calendar stone. It includes signs for twenty tonalpohualli days. But it was not a calendar. Instead, it was probably used as an altar in Aztec ritual sacrifices.

When the Sun Stone was first discovered in Mexico City, Mexico, in 1790, people thought it was an Aztec calendar. Hieroglyphs carved on the stone refer to special days in the Aztec year. The stone was probably used as an altar.

The Aztecs believed that their gods, including the sun god, required frequent offerings of blood. Human sacrifice was a common ritual to keep the Sun shining and keep the heavens in order.

INCAN COUNTING ROPES

The Incas of South America were a thriving society from about A.D. 1400 to 1600. Nestled in the Andes Mountains, the Incas did not interact with European or Asian civilizations until the Spanish arrived in the 1500s. The Inca culture developed unaware of the advancements made in earlier times in Central America.

The Incas are known for their impressive building feats. They built Machu Picchu, an ancient city on a steep mountain ridge in Peru. They are not known for their mathematical advances. But like the Egyptians, the Incas would have needed computing to keep building projects in order and keep records of workers, supplies, and land. However, most experts believe that the Incas had no writing system. Information probalby was passed through word of mouth. So how did they save information? They used the quipu, a group of knotted cords that served as a complex recording device for numbers. Quipus kept track of people counted in a census, a farmer's animals, tax records, and more.

A quipu had a main horizontal cord with several vertical cords attached to it. Other cords may have been attached to some of those cords, like small branches attached to larger branches on a tree. The Incas recorded information on quipus by tying knots on each cord. Knots of three types and in different points along a cord stood for numbers in different place values, such as hundreds, tens, or ones. Cords of different colors were used to identify the things being counted. One color may have stood for sheep and another color for llamas, for example. The end cord may have shown the total when the other cords' numbers were added together.

Quipus, such as this one, were used by the Inca to record and store information through a system of knots. Quipus were often made from spun llama or alpaca hair. Others were made from cotton fiber.

With so much meaning coded into the rope colors and the knots, a quipu would not have meant much to someone who didn't know how to "read" it. So certain members of Inca societies were responsible for remembering and interpreting the information stored in quipus.

CHAPTER SEVEN

ANCIENT GREECE

▲ The Parthenon and other ancient Greek structures from the 400s B.C. still stand on the Acropolis, the hill overlooking the modern-day city of Athens, Greece.

Ancient Greece was a powerful civilization that conquered much of the Mediterranean and Middle Eastern worlds—from Egypt to the border of India. The Greeks founded the city of Alexandria in Egypt. It became a center for computing and science. The Greeks borrowed some computing technology from the Egyptians, but they did not just make small improvements. Instead, the Greeks developed entirely new fields of computing. They laid the foundation for modern mathematics.

To the Egyptians, math was a practical tool used for figuring taxes, conducting business, and building structures. The Greeks, on the other hand, admired math for its logic. They thought of it as a way to train the mind.

The Greeks separated math into two main branches. They used applied math to solve practical problems. Theoretical math involved the study of lines, figures, and points that do not exist in nature. The Greeks also used math to prove and disprove theories about the natural world.

GREEK NUMERALS

Imagine having to memorize twenty-seven symbols for numbers instead of the ten we use. That's what students in ancient Greece did. The Greeks used the twenty-four letters in their alphabet to stand for numbers. When they ran out of their own letters, they borrowed three letters from the Phoenician alphabet, an older alphabet from the area that is now Lebanon, Syria, and Israel.

The first nine Greek letters stood for the single-digit numbers, 1 through 9. The second nine letters represented multiples of ten—10, 20, 30, and so on up to 90. The last nine letters stood for hundreds, up to 900. A bar placed to the left of a numeral indicated thousands. The letter *M* below a numeral stood for tens of thousands.

Ancient Greeks used letters of their alphabet to stand for numbers. Greek letters and numbers are inscribed on this stone plaque, found in Ephesus (modern-day Turkey). The ancient Greeks populated Ephesus from the tenth century B.C. through 190 B.C., when it fell under Roman rule.

A FAMOUS THEOREM

The Greek philosopher Pythagoras lived from about 580 to 500 B.C. Pythagoras started a school of math and philosophy in Crotone, in modern-day Italy, which was then part of Greece. His students were called the Pythagoreans.

Pythagoras is best remembered for creating a theorem about right triangles. These are triangles that include a right (90-degree) angle. The side opposite the right angle is called the hypotenuse. Pythagoras discovered that the length of the hypotenuse, squared

The Greek philosopher and mathematician Pythagoras is honored in this relief carving on the Royal Portal of the Chartres Cathedral near Paris, France. The cathedral was built in the 1100s.

(multiplied by itself), is equal to the sum of the squares of the other two legs of the triangle. We often state the Pythagorean theorem as $a^2 + b^2 = c^2$. In this equation, a and b stand for the legs that form the right angle of the triangle, and c stands for the hypotenuse.

Although Pythagoras gets the credit for the theorem, the Babylonians knew about this equation a thousand years before Pythagoras. The Babylonians used the equation in surveying land and figuring the area of fields. The Chinese may have already known it too.

ONE THEOREM LEADS TO ANOTHER

Euclid, another Greek mathematician, taught math in Alexandria. He studied prime numbers. A prime number is one that can be divided evenly only by 1 and itself, such as 3, 7, or 11. Euclid proved that there are an infinite number of primes.

Around 300 B.C., Euclid put together many theorems about geometry, including many from other important mathematicians. He used one theorem to prove another and that theorem to prove the next. But Euclid ran into a problem. If each theorem was proved with an existing theorem, how could a person prove the first theorem? Euclid solved that problem using axioms—statements so obvious that proving them is unnecessary. Here are the five axioms (also called postulates) that Euclid used:

1. A straight line segment can be drawn to connect any two points.
2. Any straight line segment can extend to form an endless straight line.
3. Given any straight line segment, a circle can be drawn with one endpoint as its center and the line segment as its radius (the distance from the center to the perimeter of a circle).
4. All right angles are equal, measuring 90 degrees.
5. Take two lines that cross a third line. If the inner angles on one side of the third line add up to less than 180 degrees, the first two will eventually cross each other on that side. (This statement is equivalent to what is known as the parallel postulate.)

With axioms and theorems, Euclid organized a system of geometry known as Euclidean geometry in modern times. Euclid put his system into a thirteen-volume book, the *Elements*. It was used as a basic geometry textbook for two thousand years. Modern high school geometry courses are still based on the first volumes of the *Elements*.

PROOF OF THE OBVIOUS?

Although Euclid was one of the greatest mathematicians in history, some experts thought parts of the *Elements* were silly. They said Euclid wasted time proving ideas that were obvious.

▼ This page from Euclid's *Elements*, originally written in about 300 B.C., deals with triangles.

In one part, for instance, Euclid proved that no one side of a triangle can be longer than the other two sides added together. He drew a triangle with the corners labeled A, B, and C. Euclid explained that if a hungry mule stood at point A and a bale of hay sat at point B, the mule would know that the shortest route to the hay was directly from point A to point B, not from A to C to B. Epicureans, students of another Greek school of thought, made fun of Euclid for spending time proving something that was obvious even to an animal.

ANCIENT COMPUTING SCHOOL

The Greek philosopher Plato believed that society would benefit if everybody were educated to the highest level possible. This great thinker lived from about 428 to 347 B.C.

> "Geometry is the knowledge of the eternally existent."

—Plato, in *Plato's Republic*, ca. 380 B.C.

Plato was not a mathematician, but he loved math and encouraged people to study it. Many great mathematicians came to Plato's Academy, a school of philosophy and science, in Athens. Above the school's doorway, Plato put a sign: "Let no one ignorant of geometry enter here."

EUREKA!

Archimedes lived from about 287 to 212 B.C. He was the science adviser to Hiero II, who ruled the city of Syracuse on the island of Sicily, south of Italy. (Sicily was then part of the Greek world.) The Roman writer Vitruvius wrote about one of Archimedes' discoveries—a story that has become legendary. The story goes that Hiero asked Archimedes to find out whether a crown he'd had made for the gods was made of pure gold or a mixture of gold and silver. Archimedes supposedly figured out the answer while sitting in the bathtub. He leaped from the tub and ran naked through the streets shouting "Eureka! Eureka!" That's Greek for "I have found it."

According to the story, Archimedes had realized that a gold or silver object submerged in water would displace, or push aside, water equal to its own volume. (This is because gold and silver are denser than water and will sink, not float.) Since gold weighs more than silver, Archimedes knew a crown of gold and silver would displace more water than a pure gold crown that weighed the same. The gold and silver crown would be bulkier from the extra silver needed to make it weigh the same.

Archimedes dropped masses of pure gold and pure silver into water to measure the displacement. Then he dropped in the crown. Sure enough, it displaced more water than the pure gold mass had. Archimedes had figured out that the king's crown was not made of pure gold.

Modern mathematicians as far back as the Italian astronomer Galileo, in the 1600s, have doubted this story. They say this method would not make a very exact measurement. And they doubt Archimedes would have measured gold in the crown with a method that inexact, since he was so brilliant. However, Archimedes may have indeed been in the bathtub when he discovered the math principle used in the story.

THE GREATEST MATHEMATICIAN?

Some historians think that Archimedes was the ancient world's greatest math wizard. He used math to design machines and made great advances in computing technology. For example, around 240 B.C., Archimedes computed a new value for pi that was much more accurate than earlier figures. Using an arithmetic formula, he found the perimeter of a ninety-six-sided shape just barely outside the circle. Then he used the formula to find the perimeter of another shape just inside the circle. Archimedes knew the perimeter of the circle would be between those numbers. He was the first to calculate pi this way instead of with actual measurements. This approach, known as the method of exhaustion, gave him better results. He found that pi is between $3^1/_7$ (about 3.1429) and $3^{10}/_{71}$ (about 3.1408). Mathematicians used his figure for centuries.

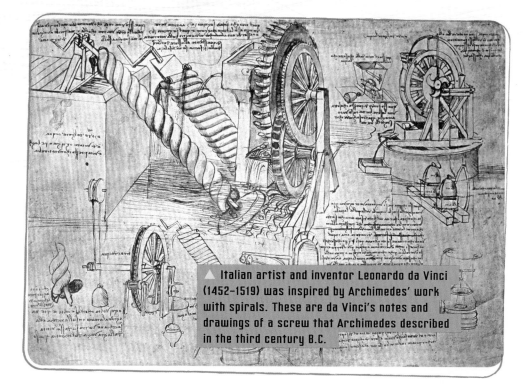

▲ Italian artist and inventor Leonardo da Vinci (1452–1519) was inspired by Archimedes' work with spirals. These are da Vinci's notes and drawings of a screw that Archimedes described in the third century B.C.

Archimedes studied spirals and figured out properties such as the surface area covered by each of a spiral's turns. In his study of spirals, Archimedes developed special math techniques. They were the basis, centuries later, for a field of math called integral calculus.

Archimedes also studied the properties of spheres and cylinders. He wrote about his discoveries in books such as *On Spirals, On Floating Bodies, On the Measurement of the Circle,* and *On the Sphere and the Cylinder.*

In one of his last works, *The Sand-Reckoner,* Archimedes calculated how many grains of sand it would take to fill the universe. He ended up with a number equal to 8 followed by 63 zeros. To find this figure, Archimedes developed a system for computing with very large numbers. It is the basis for scientific notation, a way of writing very big—and very small—numbers. In scientific notation, 894,000,000 would be written 8.94×10^8, where 10^8 is the same as a 1 followed by eight zeros.

FATHER OF ALGEBRA

Diophantus was a mathematician who lived in Alexandria around A.D. 275. Diophantus has been called the father of algebra. He introduced the use of symbols and equations (such as x + y = z) in math and wrote *Arithmetica*, the world's first book on algebra, in the third century A.D.

Arithmetica consisted of thirteen volumes and included about 130 problems. It was used for centuries. It helped engineers use algebra to measure land and construct roads and buildings.

ANCIENTS LEARNING FROM ANCIENTS

Remember how Mesopotamian astronomers used math to study the movements of heavenly bodies and to predict eclipses? In the 100s B.C., a Greek astronomer named Hipparchus also studied astronomical events.

Hipparchus learned about the Mesopotamian system of counting seconds and minutes by 60s. He used it to track the positions of heavenly bodies. He also used trigonometry to study the position of the Sun and planets and was able to more accurately measure the length of a year. His calculation was correct to within 6.5 minutes.

TICK TOCK, BETTER CLOCKS

A Greek engineer named Ctesibius of Alexandria made an early form of our modern mechanical clock in the second century B.C. It was a clepsydra, or water clock. It was more advanced than those used in ancient Egypt. Ctesibius's clock consisted of a float with a vertical rod on top. A doll-like statue, with a pointer in its hand, was attached to the top of the rod. The pointer showed the time and the date by pointing to lines on a dial. The float was placed in a container of water. It rose as water steadily dripped into the container. When the water reached the top, it flowed out to start again, and the float moved down. The pointer also moved down.

THE DECLINE OF ALEXANDRIA

The first female mathematician known by name was Hypatia *(right)*. She was born around A.D. 370. She went on to become the leader of a large group of philosophers and scientists based in Alexandria, Egypt. Hypatia wrote a number of works on mathematics, including a book on astronomy.

An angry mob murdered Hypatia in 415. Why? Nobody knows exactly. Some historians believe that Hypatia became too famous and that people envied her. Others think that the murder was part of a backlash against scientists. Some Christians said that scientists did not believe in God. The mob may have killed Hypatia for that reason.

Many mathematicians and scientists fled Alexandria after Hypatia's murder. They probably feared that they, too, would be killed. Before the murder, Alexandria had been the world's center of science, medicine, and learning for almost seven hundred years. Historians use Hypatia's death to mark the end of Alexandria as the global center of learning.

▲ This terra-cotta sculpture of Greek mathematician Hypatia was made in the A.D. 400s.

Other Greek water clocks were fancier. Their pointers were attached to gears that moved as water flowed from the clocks. The gears' movements caused polished stones to drop into bowls or little statues to spin, marking the passage of time.

ANCIENT CLOCK TOWER

Have you ever heard of Big Ben? It's a 13-ton (12-metric-ton) bell in the Clock Tower of the Houses of Parliament in London, England. People have used Big Ben to keep track of the time since 1859. The Tower of the Winds in ancient Athens held giant sundials. They were the ancient world's Big Ben. Also known as the Horologium, the Tower of the Winds is still standing. It is a marble tower 42 feet (13 m) high and 26 feet (8 m) across.

Andronicus of Cyrrhus, a Greek astronomer and mathematician, designed

▲ The Tower of the Winds helped ancient Greeks keep track of time and wind direction. The marble structure, built in 100 B.C., still stands in Athens.

the tower around 100 B.C. It has eight sides, each containing a sundial that keeps very precise time. Using geometry, Andronicus computed exactly how shadows would fall onto the surfaces of the sundials. For telling time at night and on cloudy days, Andronicus added a clepsydra inside the tower.

AN ANCIENT COMPUTER?

In 1901 divers swimming off the island of Antikythera, near Greece, found the remains of an unusual mechanical device. It came from the wreck of a

▲ This is one of the gears from the Antikythera Mechanism, which was recovered from the bottom of the sea in 1901. The device, made in the second century B.C., is a series of bronze gears that may have been used in navigation.

ship that had sunk two thousand years earlier. The device became known as the Antikythera Mechanism.

Nobody knew what the device was until the 1950s, when a Yale University scientist, Derek de Solla Price, concluded that it was an ancient computer. It had thirty gears, as well as pointers and dials. The machinery turned to calculate the rising and setting of the Sun and the Moon and movements of important stars. Professor de Solla Price thought that the Antikythera Mechanism had probably been displayed in a museum or public hall, where people could have looked at it and marveled. Maybe, he said, it had been displayed in the Tower of the Winds.

In 2005 scientists from Greece and the United Kingdom conducted new studies on the Antikythera Mechanism with cutting-edge technology. They used three-dimensional X-rays, surface imaging, and detailed digital photography to see inside the mechanism. With this new data, they explored its tiniest internal parts.

The new technology also captured images of ancient inscriptions so faint or hidden that no one had seen them since the device sank with the ship. These inscriptions shed light on the functions of the mechanism. The ancient computer predicted solar eclipses and even kept track of the four-year cycle of the ancient Olympic Games. In addition, dials on the back of the mechanism bear the names of the twelve months of an ancient calendar. The names have origins in Sicily. Scientists think these names may connect the Antikythera

▲ A reconstruction of the Antikythera Mechanism, made with the help of modern-day technology, is on display at a museum in Athens.

Mechanism to Sicily's most famous mathematician, Archimedes.

The brilliant designer behind this ancient computer is just one of its many remaining mysteries. No one developed a more advanced computing device than the Antikythera Mechanism for more than a thousand years after its creation.

THE MOTIONLESS RUNNER

Computing technology can do more than solve practical problems. It can help prove or disprove ideas about the natural world. The Greek philosopher Zeno of Elea, who lived from 495 to 430 B.C., used math to try to prove or disprove common ideas about time and space.

His ideas became known as Zeno's Paradoxes. A paradox is a statement that is contradictory or illogical. The Dichotomy was one of Zeno's most famous: Motion cannot exist because before that which is in motion can reach its destination, it must reach the midpoint of its course. But before it can reach the middle, it must reach the quarter point. But before it reaches the quarter point, it must first reach the eighthpoint, etc. Hence, motion can never start.

To understand the paradox, suppose a girl wants to run to a

This bust of Zeno was found in Herculaneum, on the southwestern coast of Italy. Zeno was a great mathematician who lived from 495 to 430 B.C. in Elea, Italy, which was once part of the ancient Greek empire.

friend 100 feet (30 m) down the street. First, she has to reach the 50-foot (15 m) mark. Before that, she has to reach the 25-foot (7.6 m) mark. To do that, she must reach the 12.5-foot (3.8 m) mark. Before that, she has to run 6.25 feet (1.9 m). Since space can be divided into an infinite (unending) number of tiny units and each unit will take a certain amount of time to cover, the girl would need an infinite amount of time to reach her goal.

This paradox may seem silly or illogical. But it created a big headache for mathematicians. For centuries no one could prove Zeno wrong. Mathematicians finally succeeded in the late 1800s. They disproved the paradox using the theory of infinite sets, which is a mathematical way of describing relationships among objects.

CHAPTER EIGHT

ANCIENT ROME

Ancient Rome began as a small town, founded in 753 B.C. and located on the Tiber River in central Italy. Gradually, the Romans conquered neighboring lands and built a great empire. It eventually stretched from the Caspian Sea and Red Sea in the east, across northern Africa to Spain in the west, and to England in the north. Like many other ancient civilizations, the Romans learned about technology from neighboring groups, including the people they conquered.

In fact, the Romans inherited much of their computing technology from the Greeks. But the Romans used math and computing in a much different

▼ This painting shows a twentieth-century artist's vision of a typical day in ancient Rome in A.D. 300. The ancient Romans were masters of engineering and architecture. Many of their structures are still standing.

way. Whereas the Greeks admired math as a way of training the mind, the Romans were practical people who applied math to real-life problems. They needed freshwater for their cities, so they used computing technology to design aqueducts, or giant water channels. Using the groma and other surveying instruments borrowed from the conquered Egyptians, the Romans constructed roads, buildings, and other structures. The Romans used math as a tool. However, they made few important mathematical advances of their own.

I, V, X, L, C, D, M

The Romans developed a numbering system in which just seven letters from the Latin alphabet and a few extra symbols could be used to write any number—from 1 to 1,000,000,000,000,000,000,000,000 or more! The Latin letter *I* stood for 1, *V* for 5, *X* for 10, *L* for 50, *C* for 100, *D* for 500, and *M* for 1,000.

Placing a small bar over the top of a number multiplied its value by 1,000. For instance, M (1,000) with a bar on top meant 1,000,000. In theory, a person could add enough bars to write huge numbers. In practice, the Romans rarely used more than one bar.

Roman numerals were written from left to right. A number placed to the right of another number of equal or greater value indicated addition. That is, VI meant 5 + 1, or 6. MD meant 1,000 + 500, or 1,500. DC meant 500 + 100, or 600. A number placed to the left of another number of greater value indicated subtraction. For example, XL meant 50 – 10, or 40. DM meant 1,000 – 500, or 500. MCM meant 1,000 + (1,000 – 100), or 1,900.

Try writing your street number, height, and weight using Roman numerals. Can you guess the big disadvantage? For one thing, the numbers can take up a lot of space. They are also hard to use for addition, subtraction, multiplication, and division.

EVERYONE'S FAVORITE COMPUTER

By the first century B.C., the abacus was a common counting and calculating tool in ancient Rome—long before it gained popularity in China. The Romans used some abacuses with rods, like the Chinese. Another Roman version had grooves in which pebbles or smooth, round metal counters could be moved.

▲ This bronze abacus is from ancient Rome.

HOW FAR HAVE WE COME?

In modern cars, an odometer in the dashboard shows how far the car has traveled. It may be surrounded by state-of-the-art screens and buttons at the driver's fingertips, but the odometer is actually ancient technology. The first odometer was developed by Marcus Vitruvius Pollio, a Roman engineer. He lived from 70 to 25 B.C. He mounted a large wheel in a frame, much like a modern wheelbarrow. The wheel was attached to a gear with four hundred notches. With each turn of the wheel, the gear moved ahead one notch. The gear moved four hundred times every five thousand Roman feet, equal to one Roman mile. And with each four hundred turns, a stone dropped into a metal container. The clang of the stone signaled that one Roman mile had passed.

Vitruvius envisioned using the device in chariots and wagons so that travelers could measure distance. At the end of each day's travel, a driver

This reconstruction of an ancient Roman odometer was created based on the descriptions of the device by the Greek mathematician Heron of Alexandria, Egypt (a Roman city at the time), and Roman Marcus Vitruvius Pollio. The men lived around the same time in the first century B.C.

A ROMAN MILE

For long distances, Romans used the measurement known as *mille passuum*, or one thousand paces. This distance was equivalent to five thousand Roman feet. It is also known as one Roman mile. In modern measurements, a Roman mile is about 0.92 modern miles, or 1,479 m. The Romans used this measurement in constructing canals, roads, protective walls and forts for the army, and more.

▲ A Roman road and arched gate built in the second century A.D. still stand at al-Bas, in modern Lebanon.

could count the number of stones in the container, tally his mileage, and reload the stones for the next day's journey.

BETTER CALENDARS

The first Roman calendar, developed around 738 B.C., was based on the lunar year. With just 304 days—divided into ten months—the calendar was 61 days

> ## "Geometry was in high esteem with [the Greeks], therefore none were more honorable than mathematicians. But we [Romans] have confined this art to bare measuring and calculating."

— Marcus Tullius Cicero, Roman philosopher and politician, in *Tusculan Disputations*, bk. 1, ca. 45 B.C.

short. Later, the Romans added two more months, but they were not long enough. To make up for the shortfall, the Romans had to add an extra month to their calendar every two years.

The Roman calendar got further off track when officials started adding even more extra months. Why? Sometimes they did it to stay in office longer or delay elections. Finally, in 45 B.C., Emperor Julius Caesar adopted the Egyptian solar calendar for the Roman Empire. He called it the Julian calendar in his own honor. It had a year of 365 days and every fourth year—leap year—an extra day. The Julian calendar was very accurate. It was only eleven minutes, fourteen seconds longer than the solar year.

▲ A Julian calendar carved into stone has pegs marking the month *(center)*, date *(sides)*, and day of the week *(top)*. The Julian calendar was used in ancient Rome.

AFTER THE ANCIENTS

Ancient societies rose and fell. Often, groups grew politically or economically weak, and stronger groups conquered them. But even after a culture died out, its technology often remained. Conquering groups built on the knowledge of conquered peoples to further develop technology.

This wasn't always the case, however. After the Roman Empire fell to invaders in A.D. 476, Europe entered a period called the Middle Ages (about 500 to 1500). The early Middle Ages are sometimes called the Dark Ages, because art, culture, and learning were minimal in Europe during these years. Few people in Europe went to school. Few craftspeople knew about or improved upon ancient technology. Around 900, Hindu-Arabic numerals made their way into Europe. They replaced Roman numerals for everyday use, setting the stage for easier calculating with the Indian decimal system.

Cultures in other parts of the world continued to develop their understanding of computing and mathematics during the Middle Ages. The Maya flourished in Central America. In China the Tang dynasty enjoyed many advances in civilization. The Inca of Peru built a thriving empire in the mountains.

Then, during a period called the Renaissance (1300s–1600), Europeans rediscovered the technology of ancient Greece and Rome. By the 1400s, scholars rediscovered ancient math books and scrolls stored in the libraries and monasteries of previous European empires. The

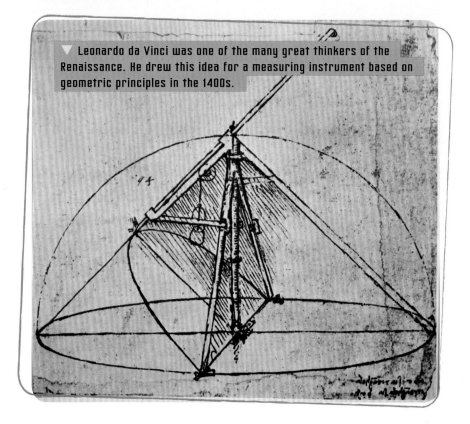
Leonardo da Vinci was one of the many great thinkers of the Renaissance. He drew this idea for a measuring instrument based on geometric principles in the 1400s.

rediscovery of advanced mathematics from ancient times jump-started modern mathematics.

In addition, global exploration spurred on the spread of technology. Europeans explored and settled in the Americas throughout the 1500s and 1600s. European colonies in Asia and Africa also brought the knowledge of different cultures together. In many places, oppressive colonial rule—or brutal conquest—meant that the less powerful group's knowledge and technology were ignored. This was the case when the Spanish conquered the Inca in South America. Nevertheless, as global mobility and communication increased, so did the spread of mathematical ideas.

TECHNOLOGY THAT ENDURED

In modern times, much of our computing technology has conserved ancient techniques. Our modern numbering system is based on the number 10. But you can find evidence of the Mesopotamian numbering system, based on 60, in our daily lives too. We still use 60 as a base measurement for time. A minute has 60 seconds. An hour has 60 minutes. Degrees (units of measurement for angles) are also based on the number 60. A circle contains 360 degrees, which is 60×6.

Beam scales are another example of ancient Babylonian computing technology that lasted. These scales are still useful for many different purposes. The scales traditionally used in doctors' offices are beam scales. The weights that slide across the top balance out your body's weight.

In some places, shopkeepers and others still use abacuses. Over time and around the globe, these simple computers have held their own against advancing technology. The Chinese were not the only culture to develop a calculator of that sort. Other versions of the abacus were used in ancient Sumeria, ancient Greece, and ancient Rome, and into modern times in Russia and Japan. The U.S. Army tested the usefulness of the Japanese abacus in 1946. It pitted the abacus against a then-new electric calculator in a contest of speed and accuracy. Each machine had a skilled operator to solve problems using addition, subtraction, multiplication, and division. The abacus won, 4 points to 1!

BUILDING ON ANCIENT IDEAS

With time, of course, people improved upon many types of computing technology. One example of this is our modern calendar. After Julius Caesar adopted the Julian calendar in 45 B.C., people in many parts of the world used it for more than 1,500 years. But over time, the eleven-minute-per-year error in the calendar had accumulated into days. Holidays were occurring at the wrong time of year.

A newer calendar, known as the Gregorian calendar, was almost exactly as long as the solar year. This calendar used the designations B.C. and A.D., based on the Christian timeline of the birth of Jesus Christ. A monk had devised this year-numbering system in 525. B.C. stands for "Before Christ." A.D. stands for the Latin words *anno Domini*, "In the year of our Lord."

In 1582 Pope Gregory XIII, the head of the Roman Catholic Church, ordered that ten days be dropped from the calendar. He adopted the Gregorian calendar. This is the calendar that is still in use in most countries.

Vitruvius's odometer also inspired improvements. The Romans had never used the odometer Vitruvius wrote about. It was forgotten for about 1,300 years. Then his design was rediscovered in 1414. The great Italian engineer Leonardo da Vinci (1452–1519) later tried to create it from Vitruvius's written description, but he could not make it work. Thanks to advances in mechanical technology, in the mid-1800s, inventors created odometers of the type used throughout the twentieth century. These odometers used multiple gears. Each gear turned a dial of digits so that a driver could see how far he or she had traveled.

By the 1600s, mathematicians introduced many other new ideas based on ancient concepts. In 1619 the French mathematician René Descartes invented coordinate geometry. He studied geometry on a coordinate (numbered) grid, using principles of algebra. This led to more advanced geometry as mathematicians could work with equations to create and change lines, planes, or shapes within the grid.

French mathematicians Pierre de Fermat and Blaise Pascal created the mathematical concept of probability in 1654. Probability involves counting the number of possible outcomes in a situation to determine how likely a certain outcome is. When you flip a coin, it can land on one of two sides. So the probability of it landing heads-up is one in two. Probability is an

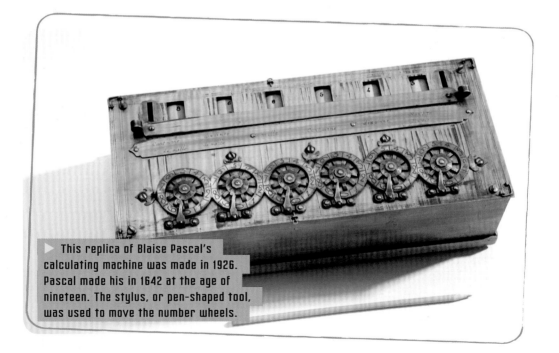

▶ This replica of Blaise Pascal's calculating machine was made in 1926. Pascal made his in 1642 at the age of nineteen. The stylus, or pen-shaped tool, was used to move the number wheels.

important concept in the modern fields of statistics, finance, science, and philosophy.

The field of calculus, the study of change, opened up a decade later. Among its many uses, calculus is used to define curves, areas, and volumes. In 1665 Isaac Newton, a British scientist and mathematician, showed how the two central operations in calculus relate to each other. The German philosopher and mathematician Gottfried Leibniz also developed this field independently of Newton. In the 1670s, he created the notation that most calculus students still learn to write equations. Calculus paved the way for countless advances in engineering and mechanics, physics, statistics, astronomy, economics, medicine, and more.

FROM MATHEMATICS TO COMPUTERS

Mathematicians have continued to build and improve on one another's ideas over time. But how did we get from calculus to laptops?

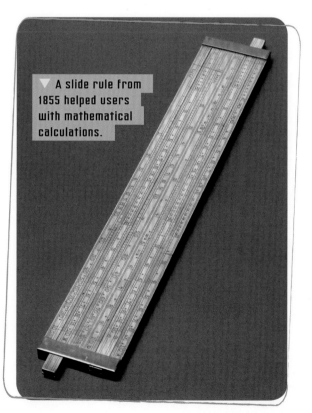

▼ A slide rule from 1855 helped users with mathematical calculations.

Abacuses and the Antikythera Mechanism were early versions of calculators or computers. So was the slide rule, a numbered sliding tool invented in the seventeenth century. The slide rule saved time and errors in calculating. A user found an answer to a calculation by positioning parts of the slide rule so certain numbers matched up.

Digital computers—such as modern computers—are programmable machines. The user can program them to perform certain operations. The first such machines appeared in the early 1800s. Early programmable machines included a textile loom and a mechanical computer.

British mathematician Alan Turing worked with computation in the 1930s. His ideas earned him the nickname the father of computer science. However, American George Stibitz is often considered the father of the modern computer. In 1937 he built the first calculator that used the binary numeral system, or binary code, to perform arithmetic. Binary code uses patterns of 0s and 1s. For example, the number 9 in the decimal system can be written as 1001 in binary code. All modern computers use binary code in their internal operations.

▼ This 1946 photo of the Electronic Numerical Integrator and Computer (ENIAC), an early electronic computer, shows programmers at work on the room-sized device.

As electronic, digital computers advanced throughout the 1900s, they grew both in capability and size. Scientists developed hardware to store information. This changed computers from calculators into data storage machines, as we know them. Room-sized computers were built throughout the 1950s and 1960s to process increasingly advanced calculations. Then, in the 1970s, the invention

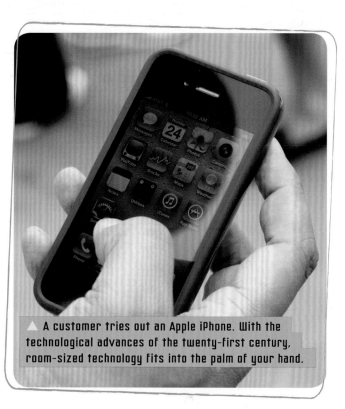

▲ A customer tries out an Apple iPhone. With the technological advances of the twenty-first century, room-sized technology fits into the palm of your hand.

of microprocessors allowed computers to shrink dramatically. By the 1980s, personal computers could fit on a desktop.

Thanks to the incredible processing ability of computers, modern people can work faster and with fewer errors than our ancestors. Computers quickly perform calculations that would take a human an entire lifetime. Because of this, they have allowed for endless developments in mathematics, science, and other fields. But none of this would be possible without the computing technology of the ancients. Their early systems for measuring, counting, and calculating gave us the tools we use every day.

TIMELINE

CA. 35,000 B.C.	Early African peoples in the modern-day country of Swaziland carve notches into a baboon bone, later known as the Lebombo bone, as a way to keep track of numbers.
CA. 3500 B.C.	Egyptians begin using obelisks as early sundials.
CA. 3000 B.C.	Mesopotamians write on clay tablets, including number symbols from their counting system based on 60. These are some of the world's earliest known number symbols.
	Egyptians begin using Nilometers to measure the water level during the Nile River's annual flood.
CA. 2000 B.C.	Babylonian and Egyptian mathematicians discover the concept of pi. They calculate the first approximate values.
CA. 1500 B.C.	Egyptians design the first clepsydra, or water clock.
CA. 1400 B.C.	Sumerians use surveying to measure land boundaries.
500S B.C.	Pythagoras proves that for any right triangle, the square of the length of the hypotenuse is equal to the sum of the squares of the other two sides. This becomes known as the Pythagorean theorem.
CA. 300 B.C.	The Babylonian astronomer Berosus creates a sundial by placing a gnomon in a bowl-shaped base. Lines on the base divide the day into twelve equal parts.
	The Greek mathematician Euclid publishes the geometry text *Elements*. This includes five axioms on which he bases some of his theorems.
240 B.C.	Archimedes uses 96-sided polygons in his "method of exhaustion" to determine that the value of pi (ϖ) is between $3\frac{1}{7}$ (about 3.1429) and $3\frac{10}{71}$ (about 3.1408).
238 B.C.	The pharaoh Ptolemy III improves the Egyptian 365-day calendar by adding one extra day every four years. The new calendar is about eleven minutes longer than the solar year.
200 B.C.–A.D. 50	The Chinese classic text *Nine Chapters on Mathematical Procedures* is written.

100S B.C.	The Greek engineer Ctesibius creates a new kind of clepsydra that is more precise and accurate than older versions.
300S A.D.	The Maya of Central America use zero as part of their base-20 numbering system.
499	Aryabhata the Elder, of India, includes tables of sine values for many angles in his book *Aryabhatiyam*.
500s	People in India begin using Hindu-Arabic numerals in a decimal system.
876	The earliest recorded zero is carved in a temple built in India.
CA. 1200	The abacus becomes popular in China, although earlier versions had existed for centuries.
CA. 1400–1600	The Inca society thrives in the Andes Mountains of South America. They use knotted ropes called *quipus* to keep records of numbers and other information.
1858	Alexander Henry Rhind finds a mathematical papyrus near Thebes, Egypt. The Rhind Mathematical Papyrus dates to about 1650 B.C.
1901	Divers find the Antikythera Mechanism among a shipwreck.
1946	The U.S. Army pits the Japanese abacus against an electric calculator in a contest of speed and accuracy. The Japanese abacus wins.
1970s	Archaeologists find the ancient Lebombo bone near Border Cave in Swaziland.
2005	Greek and British scientists study the Antikythera Mechanism with new imaging technology. They reveal inscriptions that give clues about the many uses and the origin of the mechanism.
2009	Experts at the British Library reevaluate an ancient Chinese star chart. They realize it dates to A.D. 649–684, making it the earliest known star chart.
2010	A British scientific historian cracks a "code" of mathematical patterns in Plato's ancient writings, revealing that Plato believed mathematical principles, not the gods, controlled the universe. Plato probably hid this belief to avoid punishment by religious leaders.

GLOSSARY

ALGEBRA: a branch of mathematics that deals with quantities expressed in symbols

AXIOM: a statement accepted as true that serves as a basis for further arguments or theorems

BASE-10: involving a numbering system in which place values increase in powers of 10

GEOMETRY: a branch of mathematics that deals with the measurement, properties, and relationships of points, lines, angles, surfaces, and solids

LUNAR YEAR: a time period based on the phases of the Moon, lasting a total of 354 days. The lunar year was divided into twelve months of 29 or 30 days each.

MATHEMATICS: the science of numbers

NUMERAL: a symbol used to represent a number

PI: the ratio of the circumference of a circle to its diameter; defined by mathematicians as $22 \div 7$, or approximately 3.1416

PLACE-VALUE SYSTEM: a number system in which numerals hold different values depending on their placement

PRIME NUMBER: a number that can be divided evenly only by 1 and itself

RIGHT ANGLE: an angle measuring 90 degrees

SCIENTIFIC NOTATION: a system in which numbers are expressed as a number between 1 and 10 multiplied by a power of 10. For example, 29,300 is written 2.93×10^4.

SOLAR YEAR: the time it takes Earth to make a full revolution around the Sun: 365 days, five hours, forty-eight minutes, and forty-six seconds

SURVEYING: using mathematics to measure the size and elevation of fields, mountains, valleys, and other physical formations

THEOREM: a statement in mathematics that has been proved or is to be proved

TRIGONOMETRY: the study of the properties of triangles

SOURCE NOTES

12 Ronald Schiller, "New Findings on the Origin of Man," *Readers Digest*, August 1973, 89.

21 Asger Aaboe, "Scientific Astronomy in Antiquity," *Philosophical Transactions of the Royal Society of London* 276 (1974): 41–42.

26 Ahmes the Scribe, the Rhind Papyrus, quoted in Eli Maor, *Trigonometric Delights* (Princeton, NJ: Princeton University Press, 1998), 5, available online at http://press.princeton.edu/books/maor/prologue.pdf (July 15, 2010).

32 Herodotus, *History of Herodotus*, vol. 2, trans. George Rawlinson (London: John Murray, 1862), 153–154.

33 Proclus Diadochus, *A Commentary on the First Book of Euclid's Elements*, trans. Glenn R. Morrow (Princeton, NJ: Princeton University Press, 1970).

39 Will Durant, *Our Oriental Heritage*, vol. 1 (New York: Simon and Schuster, 1954), 527, available online at http://crd.lbl.gov/~dhbailey/dhbpapers/decimal.pdf (July 14, 2010).

48 Georges Ifrah, *The Universal History of Computing* (New York: John Wiley and Sons, 2001), 24.

55 L. F. Rodríguez, *Astronomy among the Mayans* (Spanish), *Rev. Mexicana Astronom. Astrofis.* 10 (1985), 443–453, available online at MacTutor History of Mathematics, trans. John J. O'Connor and Edmund F. Robertson, http://www-history.mcs.st-and.ac.uk/HistTopics/Mayan _mathematics.html (July 14, 2010).

62 Stewart Shapiro, *The Oxford Handbook of Philosophy of Mathematics and Logic* (New York: Oxford University Press, 2005), 243.

77 "Cicero's Tusculan Disputations," Project Gutenberg, 2005, http://www .gutenberg.org/files/14988/14988-h/14988-h.htm (September 14, 2010).

SELECTED BIBLIOGRAPHY

Adkins, Lesley, and Roy A. Adkins. *Handbook to Life in Ancient Rome.* New York: Facts on File, 1994.

Asimov, Isaac. *Asimov on Numbers.* Garden City, NY: Doubleday, 1977.

Benson, Elizabeth P. *The Maya World.* New York: Thomas Y. Crowell Company, 1977.

Fauvel, John, and Jeremy Gray, eds. *The History of Mathematics: A Reader.* New York: Macmillan, 1987.

Fleet, Simon. *Clocks.* London: Octopus Books, 1972.

Grimal, Nicolas. *A History of Ancient Egypt.* Cambridge, MA: Blackwell Publishers, 1994.

Heilbron, J. L. *Geometry Civilized: History, Culture and Technique.* New York: Oxford University Press, 1998.

Hodges, Henry. *Technology in the Ancient World.* New York: Alfred A. Knopf, 1977.

Hollingdale, Stuart. *Makers of Mathematics.* New York: Penguin Books, 1991.

Ingpen, Robert, and Philip Wilkinson. *Encyclopedia of Ideas That Changed the World: The Greatest Discoveries and Inventions of Human History.* New York: Penguin Books, 1993.

James, Peter, and Nick Thorpe. *Ancient Inventions.* New York: Ballantine Books, 1994.

Novikov, Igor D. *The River of Time.* Cambridge: Cambridge University Press, 1998.

O'Connor, John J., and Edmund F. Robertson. "History of Mathematics." MacTutor History of Mathematics. May 2010. http://www-history.mcs .st-and.ac.uk/HistTopics/Mayan_mathematics.html (September 14, 2010).

Robinson, Andrew. *The Story of Writing.* New York: Thames and Hudson, 1995.

Saggs, H. W. F. *Civilization before Greece and Rome.* New Haven, CT: Yale University Press, 1989.

FURTHER READING

Asimov, Isaac. *Astronomy in Ancient Times.* Milwaukee: Gareth Stevens Publishing, 2006.
This title explores the methods and instruments that ancient astronomers used to study the sky.

Hightower, Paul. *The Father of Geometry: Euclid and His 3-D World.* Berkeley Heights, NJ: Enslow Publishers, 2010.
Get a glimpse of one of the world's first mathematicians through this look at his work, the *Elements.*

McCallum, Ann. *The Secret Life of Math: Discover How (and Why) Numbers Have Survived from the Cave Dwellers to Us!* Nashville: Williamson Books, 2005.
Read about the role math and numbers played in the ancient world through modern times.

Passport to History series. Minneapolis: Twenty-First Century Books, 2001–2004.
In this series, readers will take trips back in time to ancient China, Egypt, Greece, Rome, and the Mayan civilization. They will learn about people's clothing, medicine, work, tools, and other aspects of daily life.

Unearthing Ancient Worlds series. Minneapolis: Twenty-First Century Books, 2008–2009.
This series takes readers on journeys of discovery, as archaeologists discover King Tut's tomb, the royal Incan city of Machu Picchu, the ruins of Pompeii, and other archaeological treasures.

Visual Geography Series. Minneapolis: Twenty-First Century Books, 2003–2011.
Each book in this series examines one country, with lots of information about its ancient history. The series' companion website—Vgsbooks. com—offers free, downloadable material and links to sites with additional information about each country.

WEBSITES

Calendars through the Ages
> http://www.webexhibits.org/calendars/index.html
> Since the beginning of human history, people have measured the
> passage of time. This kid-friendly site explains how as it explores
> calendars from around the world—from both ancient and modern times.

Science Kids at Home
> http://www.sciencekidsathome.com/science_experiments/sundial-1.html
> This site gives step-by-step instructions on how to make your own
> sundial. You can tell time just like the ancients did!

Secrets of Lost Empires
> http://www.pbs.org/wgbh/nova/lostempires/
> This companion website to the PBS television series *NOVA* investigates
> architectural mysteries of the ancient world, from the grand obelisks of
> Egypt to the complex Roman water system.

Science Channel
> http://science.discovery.com/
> Use the search box on this page to search for "What the Ancients
> Knew." Then check out hundreds of video clips that explain how ancient
> civilizations used mathematical and scientific principles to accomplish
> amazing feats.

INDEX